China

Author	Linda Milliken
Illustrator	Barb Lorseyedi

EP069 ©Highsmith® Inc. 1995, 2003, 2007
W5527 State Road 106, P.O. Box 800
Fort Atkinson, WI 53538

Table of Contents

The Hands-on Heritage series has been designed to help you bring culture to life in your classroom! Look for the "For the Teacher" headings to find information to help you prepare for activities. Simply block out these sections when reproducing pages for student use.

China

No one knows for sure when people first came to the land now called China. Its written history goes back about 3,500 years, making it the world's oldest living civilization. Its visual arts date from about 4,000 B.C. The Chinese call their country *Chung Kuo*, which means *Middle Country*. This name may have come into being because the ancient Chinese thought of their country as both the geographical center of the world and the only truly cultured civilization. The name *China* was given to the country by foreigners. It may have come from *Ch'in*, which was the name of an early Chinese *dynasty*, or family of rulers.

In early times, the Chinese people were divided into many small states. In 221 B.C. the Qin dynasty established an empire with a strong central government. This empire lasted in some form for more than 2,000 years. Important inventions were developed. Great cities were built. Magnificent works of art and literature were created. During the 1800s, the Chinese empire began to weaken. In 1911, revolutionaries overthrew the Manchu dynasty and China became a republic the following year. In 1949, the Chinese Communist Party, led by *Mao Zedong*, set up another government system, the *People's Republic of China*. Nationalists fled to the island of Taiwan where they reestablished their own government.

China is the most populated country in the world. Most Chinese people belong to the Han nationality, which has been the largest in China for centuries. The rest of the population consists of about 50 minority groups, including Kazakhs, Mongols, Tibetans, and Uigurs.

Family life is extremely important in Chinese culture. Before 1949, the ideal was five generations living under one roof. But family relationships have changed through the years. In the past, children were expected to obey their parents at all costs. A father could legally kill his children if they disobeyed him. In some cases, daughters were killed at birth because girls were considered useless. Today, all children, girls as well as boys, are valued, and parents no longer expect their children to show unquestioning obedience.

Although the ancient imperial system ended in 1912, the People's Republic of China has maintained many of the great traditions and festivals and still has a strong commitment to art and literature.

Geography

China is the third largest country in the world in area. Its vast land area includes some of the world's driest deserts (Gobi), highest mountains (Mt. Everest), longest rivers (Yangtze), and most populated cities (Shanghai). China can be divided into eight major land regions, including the Tibetan Highlands and the Mongolian Uplands. China is home to about one fifth of the world's population. Five percent of its population is made up of minorities, many of whom live in the border regions and far western parts of the country. About 75 percent of China's citizens live in rural villages and small towns, with the remainder living in crowded cities.

Project
Fill in a map of China that shows some of its geographic regions, cities, landmarks, and features.

Materials
- reference books
- map of China
- construction paper
- crayons
- scissors
- glue

Directions
1. Fill in the map of China, coloring regions and features, using the map transparency as a guide. Use reference books to add at least two additional geographical details to your map as well as the cities of Shanghai and Hong Kong.

2. Cut out your map and mount on construction paper for display. Share any additions you made with the class.

For the Teacher
Copy one map of China (page 5) per student. Make a transparency of the map below to display on an overhead projector.

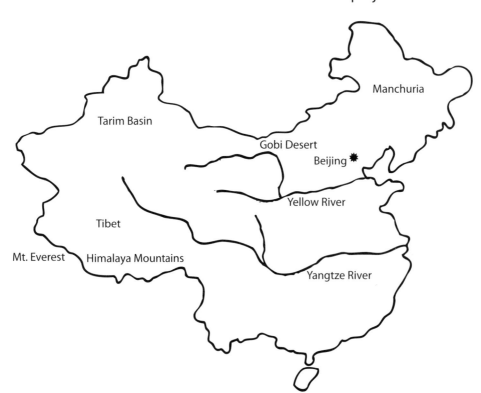

EP069 China © Highsmith® Inc. 2007

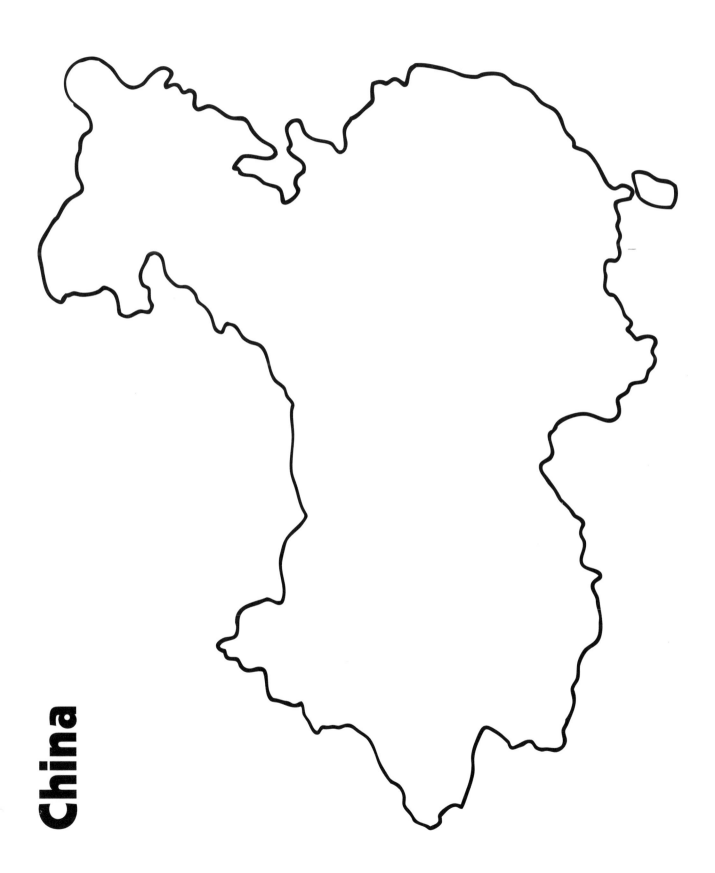

China

Great Wall of China

One of China's best-known monuments is the Great Wall. The wall was first built during the Qin Dynasty (221–226 B.C.) to keep invaders from coming into China from the north. Later, during the Ming Dynasty (A.D. 1388–1644), a major reconstruction of the wall was done. The purpose of this newly renovated wall was also to keep out invaders. This is the wall that still exists today.

The Great Wall is not one continuous wall, but many different sections with some gaps in between. Some, but not all, of these gaps are filled by mountains and impassable terrain. The exact length of the wall is unknown, but it is estimated to be around 1,500 miles (2,400 km) long. Sections are about 25–30 feet (7.6–9.1 m) high and consist of the wall itself, guard stations, and watchtowers.

Today, the Great Wall of China is one of China's most popular tourist attractions and is also the subject of many myths. The most popular myth is that the Great Wall can be seen from the moon. While it can be seen from low altitudes in Earth's atmosphere, it is not possible to see it from the moon.

Project
Try some fun activities to imagine the length of the Great Wall of China.

Materials
- walking shoes
- map of the United States

Directions
1. With an adult, measure the distance in feet it takes to walk around your school. How many times would you need to make this walk to equal the distance of the Great Wall?

2. Find your city or town on a map of the United States. Measure a distance of 1,500 miles in several directions. What state/city would you end up in? How long do you think it would take you to walk there?

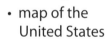

Hand-Counting

Chinese people often visit outdoor marketplaces to purchase the food and goods they need. The marketplace is a busy, noisy hub of activity. The Chinese have a system of indicating the numbers 1 to 10 with the fingers on one hand. This is very useful where signing may be more effective than shouting the number of items one wants to purchase.

Project
Learn to count to 10 in the Chinese manner by using the fingers on one hand.

Materials
- paper
- pencil

Directions
Practice counting to 10 using the chart below.

For the Teacher
Copy one hand-counting chart (below) per student.

One	Two	Three	Four	Five

Six	Seven	Eight	Nine	Ten	

Clothing

In ancient China, there were two types of clothing—one for peasants and one for rulers and the wealthy. Field workers and farmers wore very simple clothing—short tunics tied at the waist with trousers that came just below the knee. The wealthy people of ancient China wore skirts and robes made of dyed silk *embroidered* with designs. Flat-heeled shoes and gloves of silk adorned their feet and hands. Men wore hats; women went bare-headed but fashioned their hair in elaborate styles held in place with long pins and jeweled combs. An emperor's robes were highly decorative and had ceremonial significance. On the longest night of the year, a blue robe was worn; on the longest day, the robe was yellow. One of 12 dragon symbols was commonly embroidered on the robe to denote power, knowledge, fertility, and well-being.

Project

Make a sample dragon robe worn by emperors in ancient China.

Materials

- yellow and blue butcher paper
- tempera paint
- pencils
- paintbrushes

Directions

1. In cooperative groups, cut out the shape of an emperor's robe from yellow or blue butcher paper. (See illustration to the right.)
2. Sketch one or several dragons on the robe. Paint the dragon and allow it to dry.
4. Surround the dragon with swirls of bright paint in various colors.

For the Teacher

Divide class into groups of three or four. When robes are complete, hang them along the wall of the classroom.

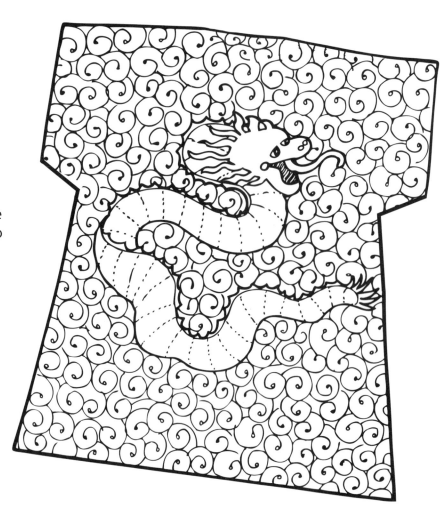

EP069 China © Highsmith® Inc. 2007

Herbs

Early Chinese people discovered that combinations of certain herbs relieved ailments. During the T'ang dynasty, a major revision was made on an earlier pharmacy reference book. This information served as the basis for one of the most respected and widely used Chinese books on the subject today. Brews of herbs, leaves, bark, and berries are cooked for hours before being drunk from bowls. More exotic items such as animal horns, dried snakes, lizards, and fat glands from the Manchurian frog are added for a stronger brew. Mint is used for relieving headaches. Scrapings of rhinoceros horns cool a fever, and tiger bone wine cures aches and pains.

The Chinese pharmacy consists of a large hall with counters on all sides, behind which are drawers, each holding an herb. Prescriptions are made by combining the different herbs.

For the Teacher

Project

Simulate a Chinese pharmacy in the classroom. Brew peppermint tea to sample.

Materials

Pharmacy

- resource books about medicinal herbs and Chinese medicine
- shoeboxes
- small pads of paper
- markers
- small plastic bags

Tea

- peppermint tea
- cups
- tea pot
- hot plate
- water

Directions

1. To simulate the pharmacy, arrange two parallel tables. Stack one with shoeboxes labeled with names of herbs found during a research session. Add some unusual ingredients as well, using those mentioned above.

2. Fill each box with imaginary herbs. Twigs, leaves, pebbles, and aquarium rocks are suggestions for use as "mock" herbs. The students can suggest other imaginative substitutions.

3. Have students take turns role-playing the patient, the doctor who writes the prescription (combination of herbs) on the pad of paper, and the pharmacist who fills the prescriptions.

4. At the close of the simulation activity, brew some peppermint tea to enjoy together.

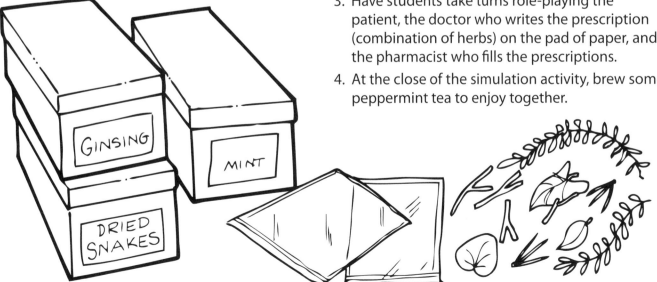

Inventions

It is believed that the Chinese were the first to invent paper made from pulp. Printing surfaces were already being made from silk fibers, but this method was expensive. An experiment in A.D. 105 with rags and plants mashed with water evolved into pressed sheets of paper. By A.D. 700, printing techniques had advanced to woodblock printing.

Many Chinese inventions came from everyday experiences. Examples include the wheelbarrow, horse collar, odometer, waterwheel, umbrella, eyeglasses, silk, mechanical clock, paper money, earthquake detector, and kites. Others, such as the compass and gunpowder, may well have changed history.

For the Teacher

Project

Have students review the Invention Presentations and choose one or several to complete.

Materials

Provide materials needed for each project as listed on the Invention Presentations page.

Directions

1. Divide class into cooperative groups of three or more students.

2. Copy one Invention Presentations (page 11) per group. Give each group the opportunity to select a presentation to complete.

3. Set a time limit for completion, then provide time for each group to present its findings.

   EP069 China © Highsmith® Inc. 2007

Invention Presentations

Compass

The maritime compass was first used more than 2,000 years ago, when the Chinese discovered that magnetite would point to a north-south direction automatically. This enabled long-distance sea travel.

Give several examples of instances where a compass is used. Take classmates on a short hike in which the compass is used and directions are called out as the hike progresses.

Wheelbarrow

Toiling in the fields meant moving materials and tools to different places. In order to make better use of time, a wheeled cart was invented.

Demonstrate a wheelbarrow's advantages in a race. Gather two piles of 10 identical things. Some should be small, some large. At a signal, one person using just his or her hands and arms and the other person using a wheelbarrow tries to move their piles to a finish line.

Umbrella

Some simple Chinese inventions have proven through time to make life easier and more enjoyable. Some examples are paper, umbrellas, eyeglasses, mechanical clocks, and kites.

Present an oral demonstration that shows the benefits of the Chinese inventions listed above. Use actual examples that show life with and without these inventions.

Earthquake Detector

The many earthquakes that struck China made it necessary to create a way to detect them. This was achieved in A.D. 132 with a bronze vase made of eight carved dragons, each with a ball in its mouth. The balls fell when the earth trembled!

Find out how earthquakes are detected and recorded now. Use pencil and paper to demonstrate how a seismograph works.

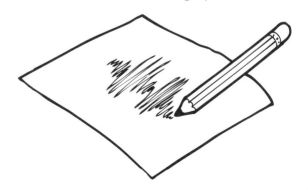

Transportation

During the Han and T'ang dynasties, wealthy families traveled in *sedan* chairs carried by two men. For the poor, the most useful vehicle was probably a wooden wheelbarrow. People of modern China often carry loads in the same way their ancestors would have 2,000 years ago. Wooden carts serve as load haulers. Large barges still carry heavy cargo along the rivers. While railroads have been built and some roads have been paved, most people still travel by bicycle or on foot. The rugged terrain in China has always made the building of roads for different transportation difficult.

For the Teacher

Project

Play some games based on the different modes of transportation in ancient and modern China.

Materials

- two wheelbarrows
- two buckets
- paperback books
- two large stuffed animals
- paper
- two chairs with arms

Directions

1. Set up stations for all transportation games. Copy the directions for each game (below and the Transportation Games page, 13) and post at each station. Provide the materials needed.

2. Explain the games and safety rules to the students.

3. Divide class into smaller groups, if desired, and rotate the groups from one game to the next until they have participated in all. Adult supervision will be needed at each game station.

Courier

In ancient China, message couriers traveled from station to station, delivering messages as they went.

Divide class into four-member teams. Position the teams in two large rectangles of equal size with a student at each corner. Give one student on each team a folded letter. At the starting signal, the student with the letter races clockwise to the next person, or courier, in the rectangle. The race continues until all couriers have carried the letter and the last one is back to the starting point. See how quickly this can be accomplished.

EP069 *China* © Highsmith® Inc. 2007

Transportation Games

Load Carrier

People still haul loads by balancing them on sticks carried across their shoulders as they did 2,000 years ago.

Hang a bucket on each end of the dowel. The first team to balance the load by filling each bucket with four or more paperback books is the winner!

Sedan Chairs

The wealthy people of ancient China rode in sedan chairs held by long, strong poles. The chair was lifted by male servants and carried to its destination.

Put two dowels through the chair arms. Set a large stuffed animal in the seat. At a signal, two players on opposite sides of the chair lift it by the poles and carry it to a finish line. At that point, the chair is carried back to the start by two other players. Repeat until all team members have a turn. If the passenger (the stuffed animal) tumbles from the seat, the players return to their starting point.

Wheelbarrows

Wooden carts and the invention of the wheelbarrow enabled people to stack and haul loads of goods.

The first team to fill a wheelbarrow with the highest load (books, jackets, stuffed animals, etc.) and move it 12 feet (4 meters) without anything falling off is the winner.

Martial Arts

The Chinese have been practicing some form of martial art for thousands of years. Traditionally, the purpose of martial arts was combat and self-defense. Today, it can be a sport as well as the basis for many forms of Chinese exercise. Most martial arts stress control, concentration, and balance. Even those that incorporate a form of kickboxing stress beauty rather than fighting. Three main types of Chinese exercise are *tai chi chaun, qigong,* and *wushu.* They are explained further below.

Project

Spend a few moments each morning practicing a form of Chinese exercise.

Materials

- clock timer
- exercise instructions

Directions

1. Review the different types of Chinese exercise.
2. Set the timer and do four minutes of one form of exercise. Rotate the exercises daily.

WUSHU

Wushu is a form of exercise-fighting practiced as self-defense. The moves of wushu are often used as exercise. There many different forms of wushu, but the focus is on strength. One form focuses on vigorous, athletic movements, incorporating hand movements and low leg stances. Another form uses slow, relaxed movements and is often done by less athletic people. Develop some moves that would fit into either of these forms of wushu and include them in your exercise program.

TAI CHI

Tai chi chuan, known as tai chi, combines graceful, circular movements with deep breathing. Basic exercises in tai chi have unusual names such as "Grasp the Bird's Tail" and "Wave Hands Like a Cloud." With these names in mind, develop some controlled moves to use in your exercise program.

QIGONG

Qigong involves deep breathing exercises aimed at achieving longevity by regulating the mind, body, and breath. Qigong can be directed to various parts of the body to increase strength, decrease pain, and control disorders such as high blood pressure. Practice some deep breathing while focusing concentration on a particular body part.

EP069 China © Highsmith® Inc. 2007

Bronze Coins

Early Chinese people traded with one another by exchanging products such as pottery, vegetables, fruit, meat, cloth, silk, weapons, and grain. This *bartering* continued until people found it more convenient to use money. During the Ch'in dynasty (221 B.C.), bronze discs with a square hole in the middle were used by everyone in the empire, along with some spade- and knife-shaped pieces.

The round coins were worth 50 units. The knife-shaped pieces equalled 500 units. The square hole in the center of each enabled them to be strung together, often in hundreds, to make carrying them easier.

Project

Make replicas of ancient Chinese coins to use in math and bartering activities.

Materials

- brown and red tempera paint, mixed to create a rusty bronze shade
- paintbrushes
- scissors
- yarn or string
- large index cards
- pencils
- Coin Patterns

Directions

1. Cut out the coin patterns, then trace them onto index cards. Cut out the shapes, including the center section. Make at least 15 round and 12 knife coins.
2. Paint both sides of the coins. When dry, string onto lengths of cut yarn.

For the Teacher

Copy one of each coin pattern (below) per student.

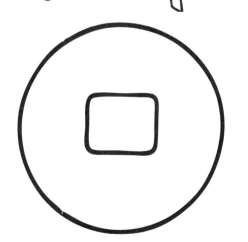

Activity Suggestions

- Plan a bartering activity. Have students bring old items to sell. They can set their own prices (in multiples of 100), barter for final costs, and exchange their coins.

- Use the coins for addition and subtraction problems, counting, and place value lessons.

Coin Patterns

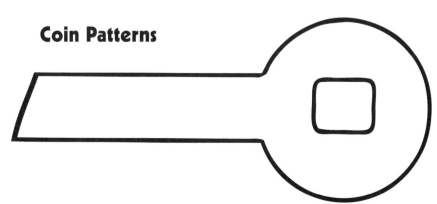

Oracle Bones

Chinese writing dating back around 3,500 years has been found scratched onto the surface of animal bones and tortoise shells. These inscriptions, called *oracle bones*, were used by *diviners*, people who try to tell the future, to answer questions put to them by the king. Some questions were about ordinary topics, like how to cure a toothache or when to hunt. Other people asked how to win on the battlefield.

After the inscriptions were scratched, the diviner applied heated metal rods that caused cracks to appear. These cracks were then interpreted to see what the answers were to the questions that had been asked.

The Chinese writing characters used today developed from these early pictures.

Project

Create a replica of an oracle bone.

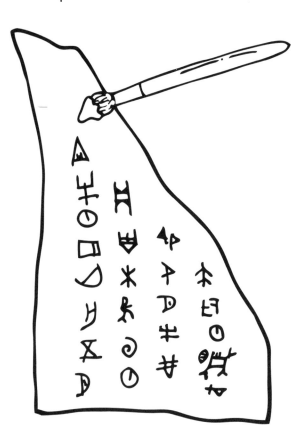

Materials

- brown paper bag
- starch
- wide-bristle paintbrush
- scissors
- light-colored crayons (white, pink, yellow)
- watercolor paints and brush

Directions

1. Cut open the paper bag and lay it flat. Cut a large, irregular shape from the bag.
2. "Paint" the irregular shape with starch and allow to dry and stiffen overnight.
3. Use the crayons to write your own picture symbols on the stiffened bag.
4. Brush the entire bag shape with a brown watercolor wash to make the symbols appear scratched on the surface.

EP069 China © Highsmith® Inc. 2007

Chinese Writing

The Chinese are believed to have the oldest written language in the world. It is made up of *pictographs* and *ideographs*. Pictographs use symbols to represent people and things. Ideographs use symbols to represent abstract ideas. Each symbol, or character, represents a complete word or syllable. Chinese written language, which has grown over the years, now consists of as many as 80,000 characters. A person who knows about 3,500 of the most frequently used characters can read a Chinese newspaper or modern novel.

Characters have changed from ancient to modern times. A simple ideograph consists of only one character. There are 11 basic strokes that are written in proper sequence. The simplest word has one stroke, while the most complicated has up to 64 strokes.

Project
Create a decorative border for the classroom using a combination of existing Chinese and your own pictographs and ideographs.

Materials
- paper
- pencil
- scratch paper
- paintbrushes
- Writing Characters page
- half-sheets white construction paper
- red and black tempera paint
- masking tape

Directions
1. Using the Writing Characters page, practice writing the characters on scratch paper. Create several original characters as well.

2. Choose two characters to recreate with paint. One should be from the Writing Characters page, the other should be an original.

3. Paint each character with red or black paint on the construction paper. Write the translation in paint underneath the character.

4. Create a decorative border on the classroom wall by taping the painted characters side by side. Use them as a reference for other Chinese writing activities.

For the Teacher
Copy one Writing Characters page (18) per student.

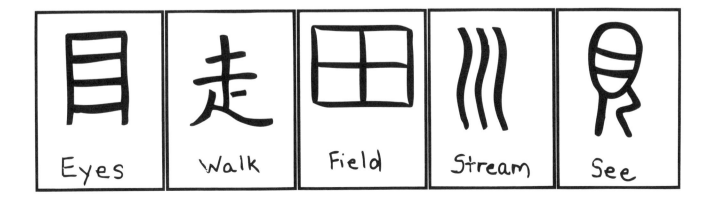

Writing Characters

日	月	車	馬
sun	**moon**	**vehicle**	**horse**
人	心	木	目
human	**heart**	**tree**	**eyes**
魚	口	狗	于
fish	**mouth**	**dog**	**hand**
去	田	見	巛
go	**field**	**see**	**stream**
母	父	作	走
mother	**father**	**make**	**walk**

EP069 China © Highsmith® Inc. 2007

Wood Writing

Before the Chinese invented paper, they recorded events and stories by writing characters from top to bottom on bamboo and wooden strips. When the strip was full, its surface would be cut off with a knife so the clean surface below could be written on.

When writing was completed on a number of strips, the strips were placed sequentially, tied together with string, and rolled into a "book." The title was written on the front of the book.

Project

Make a rolled wooden strip book that tells a story in both ancient Chinese format and in English format.

Materials

- fine-tipped markers
- wooden craft sticks (9 per project)
- scissors
- string
- clean, empty coffee (or other wide-mouth) cans

Directions

1. Review the Writing Characters page.

2. With a marker, use the Chinese characters to write a short story on the nine sticks. Remember to write from top to bottom on each stick and to place them in sequential order from left to right.

3. When your story is complete, loop string around the top and bottom of each stick and tie together as closely as possible.

4. Turn the "book" over and write a simple translation for the story across the sticks in your normal writing pattern, left to right.

5. Roll the craft sticks closed. Put them upright in cans and place the cans in the classroom library.

For the Teacher

Make sure all students have a copy of the Writing Characters (page 18). Invite students to read the ancient "books." Can they interpret the characters? Turn the "book" over and read the translation to find out.

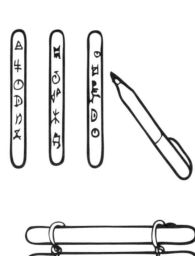

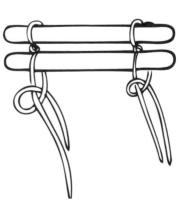

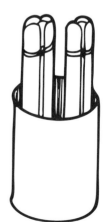

Scrolls

Many works by Chinese painters were done on silk scrolls or banners that could be rolled for storage and safekeeping. Some scrolls showed scenes from everyday life. Others, used at the head of funeral processions, showed scenes from Chinese legends depicting the journey people believed took place after death.

Artists of the T'ang period often combined fine writing, called *calligraphy*, with paintings of bamboo. The brush consisted of a wooden or bamboo handle with bristles of animal hair arranged to form an extremely fine point. They usually painted with black ink made of pine soot and glue. Vegetable or mineral pigments were sometimes added to the ink for color.

Project

Paint a Chinese scroll that features bamboo.

Materials

- long, narrow piece of white butcher paper
- paintbrush
- black tempera paint, slightly diluted
- scratch paper
- thin ribbon
- paper towels

Directions

1. Follow these steps for painting bamboo:
   - Dip the brush bristles in the diluted paint.
   - Gently press the tips of the bristles together.
   - Connect the leaves with wide vertical lines.
   - Lay the length of the bristles on the paper.
   - Turn the brush slightly before lifting it off the paper.
2. Practice the technique on scratch paper. When the technique is comfortably mastered, paint the butcher paper.
3. Display the scrolls on the classroom wall for a while. When it's time to transport them home, roll each and tie with a thin ribbon.

   EP069 China © Highsmith® Inc. 2007

Wall Posters

Big-character wall posters served as a means of communication and personal expression in China for many years. People used the posters to express their opinions. They hung them on walls in parks and other public areas. From 1978 to 1979, many people began using posters to complain about the political system. It was known as the Democracy Wall Movement. In 1980 the Chinese government outlawed the practice of hanging posters.

Communication in China comes under strict government control. Hundreds of government-published newspapers and handwritten news sheets are printed daily.

Project
Make a poster that expresses a personal opinion.

Materials
- tagboard
- markers
- crayons
- masking tape

Directions
1. Think of an opinion you have on a certain subject. Write your opinion in large letters on your piece of tagboard.
3. Decorate the poster's edges with Chinese designs.

For the Teacher
Hang all posters on the classroom wall. Use the opinions expressed on the posters as springboards to classroom discussion and debate. Discuss the phrase "freedom of expression."

Silk

According to Chinese legend, silk was discovered about 2700 B.C. when Emperor Huang-Ti ordered his wife, Lei-tzu, to find out what was damaging his mulberry trees. She found worms eating the leaves and when she accidentally dropped a cocoon into her hot tea, a slender thread unwound. Her husband looked further into Lei-tzu's discovery and developed methods that would lead to large-scale production. Silk became so valuable that the punishment for revealing the method of silk-making to a foreigner was death. The Chinese guarded their methods for almost 3,000 years.

Silk had many uses. Rich men and women in ancient China wore long silk robes held in place at the waist. Boots and shoes were also made of silk. Important documents were written on silk scrolls. Banners and flags were made from silk. Bolts of silk were valuable commodities for trading as well.

Project
Create a picture chart that shows the sequential steps in silk-making.

Materials
- Steps to Making Silk page
- white drawing paper
- crayons
- scissors
- glue

Directions
1. Color the pictures on the Steps to Making Silk page and cut them apart.
2. Glue the numbered steps in silk-making to the top of the plain white paper. Read the steps.
3. Match the pictures to the steps and arrange them in sequential order. Glue the pictures in order on the other half of the drawing paper to create a chart that illustrates the steps in silk-making.

For the Teacher
Copy one Steps to Making Silk page (23) per student.

Silk Facts
- Each cocoon may give from 2,000 to 3,000 feet (610–915 m) of filament. Four to 18 strands of this are reeled or twisted together to make a strong, even thread.
- Silk used for commerce comes from the the Bombyx mori, or mulberry silkworm, and other closely related moths.
- It is believed the first evidence of the silk trade is that of an Egyptian mummy of 1070 B.C.
- The Silk Road is the name given to the major set of trade routes between Europe and Asia.
- The word "sericulture" means the production of silk and rearing of silkworms for this purpose

EP069 China © Highsmith® Inc. 2007

Steps to Making Silk

Step 1
The leaves are picked from mulberry trees that have been cultivated by the men of the family.

Step 2
Silkworms are stored in bamboo trays on shelves and fed as many mulberry leaves as they can eat.

Step 3
The silkworm spins a cocoon.

Step 4
The cocoon is dropped into boiling water so the silk filament can be unwound.

Step 5
The thread is plucked from the hot water with chopsticks.

Step 6
The thread is twisted into strands on a spinning machine.

Step 7
Silk strands are woven together on a hand loom.

Step 8
The woven silk is washed, dyed, and hung to dry.

Zodiac

The Chinese *zodiac* moves in a cycle of 12 years, each named for an animal. Legend has it that *Buddha* once summoned all the animals of the kingdom to his bedside. Only 12 came, and in order of their appearance, he dedicated a year to each. The rat was the first, followed by the ox, tiger, rabbit, dragon, snake, horse, sheep, monkey, rooster, dog, and pig.

The people born during the year of a particular animal are said to possess certain characteristics. Review the chart on the Zodiac Comparison page to find out what years and characteristics are represented by each animal in the zodiac.

Project
Create a paper project that depicts the 12 animals in the Chinese zodiac. Learn about the characteristics of each animal and compare the personalities of classmates with their zodiac sign.

Materials
- construction paper circle, 12 inches (30 cm) in diameter
- scissors
- glue
- crayons
- Zodiac Animal Patterns page
- Zodiac Comparison page

Directions
1. Color and cut out the animal patterns.
2. Glue the animals to the outer edge of the paper circle. Begin with the rat in the 12:00 position and continue clockwise with the animals in the order shown in the illustration below.
3. Decorate the center of the paper circle with Chinese designs.
4. Complete the Zodiac Comparison page.

For the Teacher
Copy one Zodiac Animal Patterns page (25) and one Zodiac Comparison page (26) per student.

EP069 *China* © Highsmith® Inc. 2007

Zodiac Animal Patterns

Zodiac Comparison

Year 1: *Year of the Rat*—1984, 1996—Charming, bright, creative, thrifty

Year 2: *Year of the Ox*—1985, 1997—Steadfast, methodical, dependable

Year 3: *Year of the Tiger*—1986, 1998—Dynamic, warm, sincere, a leader

Year 4: *Year of the Hare*—1987, 1999—Humble, artistic, clearsighted

Year 5: *Year of the Dragon*—1988, 2000—Flamboyant, imaginative, lucky

Year 6: *Year of the Snake*—1989, 2001—Discreet, refined, intelligent

Year 7: *Year of the Horse*—1990, 2002—Sociable, competitive, stubborn

Year 8: *Year of the Sheep*—1991, 2003—Artistic, fastidious, indecisive

Year 9: *Year of the Monkey*—1992, 2004—Witty, popular, versatile, good-humored

Year 10: *Year of the Rooster*—1993, 2005—Aggressive, alert, perfectionist

Year 11: *Year of the Dog*—1994, 2006—Honest, conservative, sympathetic

Year 12: *Year of the Pig*—1995, 2007—Caring, industrious, home-loving

Choose four classmates. List each name and birth year. Find his or her animal sign and write it in the correct column. Compare his or her personality traits to those of his or her sign. Draw one or two conclusions about the similarities or differences. Write them in the conclusions column.

Name	Birth Year	Animal Sign	Conclusions
1. _____	_____	_____	_____
2. _____	_____	_____	_____
3. _____	_____	_____	_____
4. _____	_____	_____	_____

EP069 China © Highsmith® Inc. 2007

Tomb Furnishings

During the Shang dynasty (1766–1050 B.C.), ritual funerals were held for kings in which all their worldly possessions—jade, bronze weapons, ivory, pottery, mystical instruments—were buried along with human and animal sacrifices. Sometimes hundreds of people and animals were killed to accompany the dead king on his journey to the hereafter. Magnificent bronze objects decorated with mythical beasts and intricate patterns were created to bury in the main part of the tomb—a deep pit dug 30 to 40 feet (9.14 to 12.19 m) into the ground. The entrances were sometimes guarded by dead sentries armed with bronze weapons.

The practice of human and animal sacrifice ended with the Shang dynasty. Gradually, clay figures replaced people and animals. Han tombs were also richly furnished, and the walls were covered with carved stones, pottery tiles, or paintings showing happy scenes, dances, musical entertainments, meals, and processions.

Project

Make a collage that shows the worldly possessions that would be buried in your tomb in the custom of the Shang dynasty.

Materials

- construction paper
- magazines and catalogs
- personal photographs
- scissors
- glue
- paper
- pencil

Directions

1. Make an inventory list of all your worldly possessions, as well as family members and pets.

2. Use the inventory list as a checklist for gathering pictures—actual photographs, original drawings, or magazine pictures—of all possessions.

3. Arrange the possessions in a collage on construction paper. Glue in place.

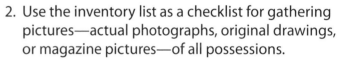

Recreation

Many of today's familiar toys such as kites, Frisbees, yo-yos, and jump ropes had their origins in China. Ancient Chinese played board games that continue to be played today. *Weiqi*, or "Go," which has been around for thousands of years, is one of the most complicated board games in the world because of the high number of possible moves. *Mah Jongg*, similar to many card games but played with tiles engraved with Chinese drawings, has been played since 500 B.C.

Sporting events are a favorite pastime in modern China. Popular sports in the country include baseball, basketball, soccer, table tennis, and volleyball.

For the Teacher

Project

Plan and participate in a "Chinese play day" that includes a variety of outdoor recreation and indoor games.

Materials

- Games and Sports (page 29)
- sporting equipment and games, as determined by students
- butcher paper

Directions

1. Involve students in planning the play day. Reproduce several copies of the Games and Sports page to distribute among them. Discuss the options, make selections, then create a "master schedule." Write it on butcher paper. Display the schedule.

2. Divide class into cooperative groups to assign responsibility for gathering the materials and equipment and setting up the various activities.

EP069 China © Highsmith® Inc. 2007

Games and Sports

Outdoor Games

Kite Flying: Kite flying has been popular in China since its invention around 200 B.C. Purchase inexpensive kites and watch them soar!

Frisbee Throwing: A favorite ancient Chinese game was disk-throwing, similar to the plastic Frisbees of today. Plan a group Frisbee toss or distance contest.

Badminton: Children in ancient China played a game similar to badminton. Provide a net, rackets, and shuttlecocks.

Chinese Jump Rope: A Chinese jump rope is similar to a large, sturdy rubber band. Two players stand opposite each other and stretch the band around their ankles while others take turns jumping in and out and making patterns with the rope. The rope starts at the ankles and is raised higher and higher with each turn.

Basketball, Volleyball: Divide into teams for a fun-filled game.

INDOOR GAMES

Leaf Game: Many Chinese games make use of natural materials. Several players may play this game. One player puts a leaf in the center of a table. Other players try to flip the leaf over by slapping their own leaf down near it. If the air current flips the leaf over, that player gets to keep his or her leaf in the center. Players take turns putting a leaf in the center.

Jacks: The original game was played with knucklebones of small animals! Learn to play with the modern metal variety.

Yo-yo: This hand-held toy originated in China. Learn how to use a yo-yo. Those who know advanced moves may teach classmates.

Table Tennis: Scale this game down to a classroom version. Obtain a standard net to suspend across a table. Use a standard ball as well, but use hands as paddles.

Gymnastics: Spread a large throw rug or mat on the floor and practice simple gymnastic moves.

Board Games: Wealthy adults in ancient China played a game similar to Backgammon. "Go" or "Mah Jongg" were also popular.

Kites

The Chinese claim that one of their generals, Han Sin, invented the kite in 206 B.C. for use in war. As kites became used for recreation, they became a form of artistic expression. Lanterns, insects, storks, flowerpots, and people are some of the shapes. Some kites have clappers and gongs, which create music when flown. All are elaborately decorated. Those with lunar designs are used in festivals.

The ninth day of the ninth month is set aside as Kites' Day. A legend tells that hundreds of years ago, a man dreamed that misfortune would strike his household. He took his family and flew kites for the day. Upon return, they found their home in ruins. The thousands of kites flown on Kites' Day celebrate this event and are supposed to float away evil spirits.

Project

Construct an unusually shaped and decorated Chinese kite to "fly" in the classroom.

Materials

- tissue paper in various colors
- tagboard or poster board
- scissors
- string
- markers
- tissue paper streamers

Directions

1. Brainstorm a list of possible kite shapes.
2. Use enlarged copies of the patterns below or cut an original shape from poster board for your kite.
3. Decorate with tissue paper and markers after the kite is completed.
4. Experiment with different shapes and tissue paper arrangements. When finished, hang your kite from the ceiling or on the wall for display. Your kite may not fly, but remember: Chinese kites are also an art form!

For the Teacher

Make enlarged copies of the shapes below for students to use as kite patterns.

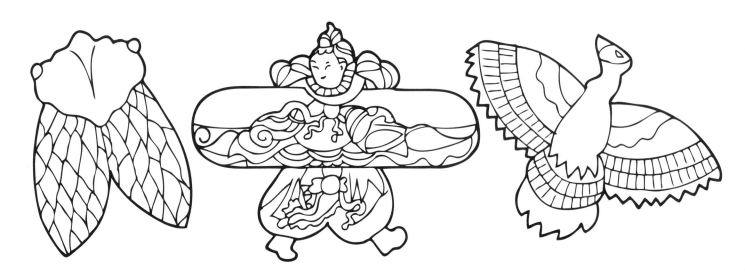

EP069 China © Highsmith® Inc. 2007

Literature

Chinese literary works, some of the world's oldest, date back about 3,000 years. Many masterpieces of Chinese literature deal with subjects such as history, philosophy, politics, religion, and science. These literary works often taught a moral lesson or expressed a political philosophy. These themes appear especially in the writings of *Confucius*, who lived from about 551 to 479 B.C.

Traditional Chinese poetry was closely associated with painting. One famous poet, Wang Wei, who lived from A.D. 701 to 761, wrote four-line poems that delicately described scenes from nature.

Project

Write a four-line poem describing a scene or subject from nature. Paint a picture to illustrate the poem.

Materials

- writing paper
- pencil
- watercolor paints and brushes
- painting paper
- various colors of construction paper
- glue or tape for mounting

Directions

1. Select a subject or theme from the list compiled by the class and write a four-line poem about it. The poem does not have to rhyme.
2. Paint a picture to illustrate the poem. Mount both to a backing of construction paper for display.

For the Teacher

Begin the project by brainstorming some themes or subjects from nature with the class. Compile the list on the board.

See the graceful bird.
It flies to its nest.
There it doesn't say a word.
It rests in its home.

Festivals

In the past, China's people held a number of festivals to celebrate holidays throughout the year. The Communist leaders of China have done away with some of China's traditional festivals and changed others to fit in more closely with their ideals. But festivals are still an important part of life in China.

Some festivals honor ancestors or historic events. May Day was established to honor working people and is now a day to encourage shopping and stimulate consumer spending. Army Day, which honors the military forces of China, is political in focus. China also observes newer holidays, such as National Day, marking the establishment of the People's Republic of China. All are celebrated with parades, demonstrations, and other traditional activities.

For the Teacher

Project

Plan a day of activities to learn about Chinese festivals and holidays.

Materials

See individual festivals, below and on the Holidays and Festivals page (33).

Directions

1. Set up three centers in the classroom, one for each festival. Stock each with the appropriate materials as well as the directions for each activity. Ask parent volunteers to help at each center.

2. Divide the class into three groups. Make a rotational schedule so that each group has time at all three centers. Allow time at the end of the day to share what was learned.

Ching Ming Festival

Usually occurs on April 4th or 5th.

During **Ching Ming**, which stands for "clean and just," families worship their ancestors by visiting the local cemetery to tidy up the graves. Afterward they often have a picnic. Sometimes offerings are made to the kitchen god, one of the most important gods worshiped by the Chinese people. They believe he rises to heaven every year to report their good and bad deeds.

Activity

Make a "good deed" mural.

Materials

- butcher paper
- crayons
- drawing paper
- glue

Directions

1. Draw a picture of a good deed you have done.

2. Glue the picture on the large sheet of butcher paper. Each group visiting the center should add their picture to the mural.

EP069 China © Highsmith® Inc. 2007

Holidays and Festivals

Dragon Boat Festival

Fifth day of the fifth lunar month

The **Dragon Boat Festival,** also called Duanwu Jie, is held to remember a patriotic poet who drowned himself because the state was taken over by a neighboring state. Dragon boat races are held and rice dumplings are eaten.

Activity

Make a dragon boat.

Materials

- cardboard milk carton
- construction paper
- scissors
- glue

Directions

1. Cut off the top of the milk carton.
2. Cut and glue construction paper on the remaining sides and bottom of the carton.
3. Create a cut-paper dragon to glue on the spout end of the carton.

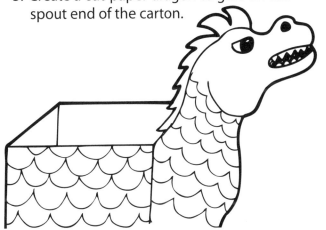

Autumn Moon Festival

Fifteenth day of the eighth lunar month.

The Autumn Moon Festival marks the time when the moon is fullest and brightest. The night is filled with lights from brightly colored paper lanterns. Moon cakes made of thin pastry filled with sweet, mashed *lotus* seeds are eaten and given as gifts.

The moon cake tradition is based on a historical event. In the fourteenth century, Chinese cooks aided their country against Mongolian conquerors by stuffing secret messages for a plan of attack inside moon cake dough. The moon cakes were widely distributed and the rebellion was a success.

Activity

Make mock moon cakes (eight to 10 per student) similar to fortune cookies. Munch on fortune cookies while making moon cakes!

Materials

- brown bags
- markers
- glue
- scissors

Directions

1. Cut bags into 4-inch (10.16-cm) squares.
2. Write a secret message or fortune inside. Fold the square twice diagonally and glue closed.

New Year

One of the most important Chinese celebrations is the New Year Festival, which marks the beginning of the new year in the Chinese lunar calendar. Festival dates vary from year to year, but always start on the first day of the first lunar month, usually between late January and late February. At the New Year, everyone becomes a year older and counts his or her age by the number of New Year celebrations he or she has seen. Celebrations last for two weeks, although some people are back at work by the fourth day. On the 15th day, a lantern festival marks the end of the celebrations. When the Communists came to power, they renamed the New Year Festival the Spring Festival. They tried to discourage many of the old customs connected with ancestor worship.

For the Teacher

Project

Have a classroom Chinese New Year celebration.

Materials

See material lists for individual activities.

Directions

1. If possible, time the activities to coincide with the dates of the Chinese New Year. Complete one activity per day.

2. Copy one set of New Year Project Pages (35–36) per student.

Spring Cleaning

The Chinese preparations start with spring cleaning, which is symbolic of cleaning out the old to make room for the new.

It's time to clean those desks, cupboards, closets, and centers! Get everyone involved in a thorough cleaning of the classroom.

EP069 China © Highsmith® Inc. 2007

New Year Project Page

Firecrackers

At midnight on New Year's Eve, firecrackers are set off to scare away the evil spirits and make a clean start to the new year.

Use a variety of bright tempera paints to make swirls, splatters, and bursts to create fireworks on a construction-paper background.

Surprise Packets

On the second day of the New Year, children kneel and pay their respects to their elders. In return, they receive little red packets with money inside.

Place a penny inside a folded piece of red paper. Tape to close. Award a packet each time a student does something kind, courteous, or respectful.

Good Luck Signs

Red signs, on which lucky sayings are written, are placed on both sides of the entry door.

Use markers to make good luck signs on red construction paper. Decorate the edges with pictographs and ideographs. Tape to classroom walls.

Paper Lanterns

On the 15th day, a lantern festival marks the end of the New Year's celebration.

Materials

- tissue paper—12. x 16 inches (30 cm x 41 cm)
- watercolor paints and brushes
- string or yarn   • scissors   • clear tape

Directions

1. Decorate the tissue paper with slightly diluted watercolor designs.
2. When the paint dries, accordion-fold the length of the tissue paper. Open and lay flat. Roll the paper into a cylinder shape. Tape the ends together. Refold the tissue paper.
3. Tape a length of string to each side of the top for hanging.

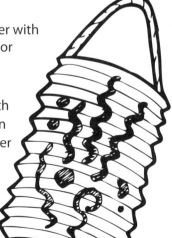

New Year Project Page

Lion Dance

Bright parades are a common occurrence during New Year celebrations. Lion dances, accompanied by cymbals, drums, and gongs, are common sights and sounds.

Construct a colorful lion mask to wear in a classroom parade.

Materials

- paper bags
- scissors
- glue
- beads, sequins, and other trims
- cereal boxes
- fabric remnants
- tempera paint
- yarn
- fringe
- paintbrushes

Directions

1. Set all materials on a common-use table.
2. Create imaginative lion masks from any or all of the materials provided.
   Each one should be original and different.
3. Display the colorful lion masks in a parade. Accompany the parade by tapping on aluminum pie tins.

EP069 China © Highsmith® Inc. 2007

Banquet

The banquet is an important type of recreation in China. On special occasions, such as weddings, lavish banquets are held with as many as 12 or more courses. An emperor's banquet, however, might consist of 132 courses at one sitting! The table is set specifically for each course. There is a saucer for soy sauce, plate, small bowl, chopsticks, spoon, and glasses.

A banquet might include roast duck, fried whole fish, stir-fried meat and vegetables, and other foods prepared and served in an elegant way. Soup is often the last dish served.

For the Teacher

Project

Work in cooperative groups to plan and carry out the preparation of a multi-course Chinese banquet, using the recipes (pages 38–39) and/or those found in Chinese cookbooks.

Materials

- Chinese cookbooks for reference
- chopsticks—available in bulk at the grocery store
- plastic spoons
- paper bowls and plates of varying size
- butcher paper
- cooking utensils and ingredients as determined by recipe selection

Directions

1. Besides planning the menu and preparing dishes, students will also be responsible for setting the banquet table.

2. Divide students into groups. Review the recipes on pages 38–39. Determine the number of courses that will be served and the responsibilities for each group. Arrange for adult assistance on banquet day.

3. Make a table covering in advance of the banquet. Cut butcher paper to fit the table tops. Decorate using markers with the students.

4. On the day of the banquet, set up areas where each group will prepare its contribution to the banquet. Appoint table setters, banquet servers, and clean-up crew. Practice using chopsticks. Enjoy!

Food

Grain is the main food source in China. Most adults eat more than 1 pound (.5 kilogram) per day. Rice is the most popular grain among people in the south. In the north, people prefer wheat, which they make into bread and noodles. Everyday meals include *fan*, which is grain, and *cai*, meaning any food cut into bite-sized pieces. *Cai* is usually vegetables, perhaps with bits of chicken, pork, or seafood. Meat makes up only a small part of the Chinese diet. Food is usually steamed or stir-fried. Meals are eaten with chopsticks and spoons—knives stay in the kitchen.

For the Teacher

Project

Prepare Chinese-style food and recipes to sample or in preparation for a multi-course Chinese banquet, page 37.

Tea

There are thousands of varieties of tea cultivated in China. While boiled water or beer may be taken with food, meals usually begin and end with tea.

Select several teas to brew and sample.

Cabbage

Chinese cabbage is one of the oldest food crops of China. It has wide, thick leaves which form long, cylindrical heads.

Finely chop Chinese or another variety of cabbage. Coat with rice vinegar.

Vegetables

The Chinese vary their diet with many vegetables especially cucumbers, eggplant, radishes, tomatoes, and turnips.

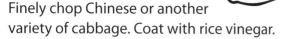

Select some vegetables to cut into thin slices or flower shapes.

Materials

See individual recipes and snack ideas.

Rice

Many meals revolve around the more than 7,000 varieties of rice grown in China.

Boil or steam rice according to package directions. Season with soy sauce.

Exploded rice looks and tastes like crispy rice cereal and is eaten as a snack or pressed together with syrup to make a cookie.

Munch on crispy rice cereal or make crispy rice treats according to package directions.

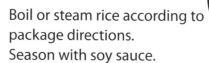

Mien (Noodles)

Chinese eat mien, or noodles, in all shapes and lengths boiled in plain soup or fried. Master noodle makers are very skilled.

Long noodles symbolize long life and are served at birthday celebrations.

Boil water and cook mien (noodles) according to package directions. Season with soy sauce. If mien is not available, cook pasta.

EP069 China © Highsmith® Inc. 2007

Recipes

Soup

Ordinary meals do not include dessert; they often end with soup. Soup may be served as a course during a banquet.

For 8 servings of egg flower soup:

Mix 2 Tbsp. (30 ml) cornstarch with 4 Tbsp. (60 ml) cold water, until the cornstarch is no longer lumpy. Beat 2 eggs separately. Boil 6 cups (1.5 ml) canned chicken broth. Add the cornstarch mixture to the soup. Stir soup until thickened. Slowly pour beaten egg into the soup. Egg will form shreds.

Fu yong

Fu yong is a pancake-type vegetable dish popular in southern China.

Combine:

- 4 well-beaten eggs
- ½ lb. (1 kg) fresh bean sprouts
- small can tuna
- thinly sliced green onion

Mix together and drop spoonfuls into heated oil in a large frying pan. Cook each pancake until lightly browned.

Stir Fry

A scarcity of fuel brought about the quick stir-frying method of cooking thinly sliced food in a wok, or bowl-shaped frying pan.

Cut beef or chicken into thin slices. Stir-fry in a small amount of oil over medium-high heat in a wok or deep frying pan.

Fruit

Every region has fruit specialties, such as bananas and oranges in the south and apples and peaches in the north.

Slice bananas, oranges, apples, and peaches. Skewer one slice of each on a toothpick.

Specialty Dishes

The Chinese are poetic about names of dishes. There is usually a story to go along with the recipe.

Ants Crawling Up a Tree Trunk

Ground meat cooked with transparent bean vermicelli.

Red-beaked Green Parrots:

Spinach served with boiled bean curd.

Monk Jumps Over the Wall:

Dried seafood stewed in a clay pot.

Have students make up their own Chinese recipe and give it an unusual name, then create a story to describe how the dish got its name.

Lacquerware

Lacquerware is made by applying varnish to such articles as trays, furniture, dishes, vases, and boxes. The process was first used during the Han dynasty (206 B.C.–A.D. 200), when lacquer was used extensively to decorate wooden objects and military equipment, such as shields.

Natural lacquer is obtained from the sap of the lac trees that grow in China. The sap is strained and dried by heat to make a dark brown liquid as thick as syrup. The liquid is diluted and sometimes colored. As many as 35 layers are applied to an object, each one thoroughly dried before the next layer is applied. Lacquerware is so durable it shows no wear for hundreds of years.

Project

Use a variation of the technique of lacquering to make a decorative box, bowl, plate, or tray.

Materials

- gift boxes of assorted sizes
- heavy-duty paper bowls and plates
- tempera paint and wide-bristle brushes
- plain newsprint
- scissors
- white glue slightly diluted with water
- empty jars or containers with lids

Directions

1. Cut out lots of shapes from the plain newsprint. These could be random shapes or Chinese-re-lated shapes, such as flowers and dragons.

2. Put some diluted white glue into each of several empty containers. Mix the glue with tempera paint to create different colors. If the glue is too thick to paint with a brush, dilute with a little more water until desired consistency is achieved.

3. Select an item to lacquer. (To make a tray, use just the lid or bottom of a box.) Place a paper shape on the item. Paint over it with the glue mixture to adhere it to the surface. One or a combination of colored glue may be used. Cover the surface

completely with "lacquered" shapes. Allow to dry for a day or more. Repeat until at least five layers have been applied.

For the Teacher

Allow a little time for students to work on the lacquerware project each day for a period of five to seven days.

EP069 China © Highsmith® Inc. 2007

Paper Cutting

The art of paper cutting dates to the Tang dynasty (A.D. 618–906). Paper cuts are used as decorations and gifts, especially during festive seasons when designs of flowers or symbols of good luck adorn lanterns and houses. Double happiness characters appear on wedding gifts, candlesticks, and incense burners. Paper cuts are also used as stencils for embroidery or prints for clothes and bed linen.

Cut-paper designs may be symmetrical or created as one unbroken piece. They are often handed down from one generation to the next and differ from village to village. Common subjects are birds, animals, and opera characters.

Project
Make a display of paper cutting samples.

Materials
- large rectangle butcher paper, any color
- various colors of plain, lightweight paper
- scissors
- glue

Directions
1. Fold the lightweight paper in half.

2. Start at the fold and make one continuous cut in the paper, being careful not to cut through the fold again until the cut is complete. Look at the illustrations for ideas.

3. When the cut is complete, unfold the paper, apply a small amount of glue, and place the cut paper on the butcher paper. Repeat as often as desired until the butcher paper is covered with paper cuts. Display.

Woodblock Print

Once paper became available, the Chinese invented printing methods. At first, bronze and stone seals were engraved with the names of important people. Ink was applied to the seal, and the name could be stamped onto paper. Eventually, less costly woodblock printing developed. As a result of this, books could be printed rather than copied by hand.

Creating a woodblock involved several steps. Characters were brushed onto paper and, while wet, were pressed on top of a woodblock covered with rice paper. When the paper was removed, a stain remained. An engraving knife was used to cut around the stain. The protruding shapes were brushed with ink. The printer smoothed paper on the inked characters to transfer the print to the paper.

Project

Make a personalized name stamp using the Chinese woodblock printing technique.

Materials

- foam plate or grocery meat tray
- wide-bristle paintbrush
- glue
- black tempera paint
- cardboard
- lightweight paper
- scissors

Directions

1. Paint your name in block letters on the paper.
2. Gently press an inverted foam plate or tray on the painted name.
3. Lift the plate and allow the paint to dry.
4. Cut around each letter.
5. Cut cardboard large enough to fit the cut letters. Glue the letters in reverse order on the cardboard, also reversing the direction the letters face. (The result will be a mirror image of the name.) Allow the glue to dry.
6. To make a final print, brush the raised letters with paint and press a piece of paper on the painted letters. Lift paper and allow to dry.

EP069 China © Highsmith® Inc. 2007

Jade

Jade has always been prized in China as the most valuable of all precious stones, cherished for its beauty and also for what was believed to be its magical properties. Because it was believed to stop bodies from decaying, a jade *pi*, or disk, was often buried with the dead. Jade burial suits were found in the tombs of the Han emperor, Liu Sheng, and his wife, Dou Wan. Together, their suits were made of 2,498 pieces of jade connected by 2.5 pounds (1.13 kg) of gold wire. During the Han and T'ang dynasties, jade worn as jewelry became a sign of wealth and power.

Jade was difficult to carve because of its hardness. Elaborate processes were developed to carve it into different shapes, such as animal figures and delicate vessels. The carvings were so fine that objects often appeared translucent.

Project
Use tissue paper and starch to create a mosaic of a jade object.

Materials
- green tissue paper in assorted shades
- starch (diluted slightly with water)
- paper cups
- paper plates
- paintbrushes
- waxed paper
- scissors

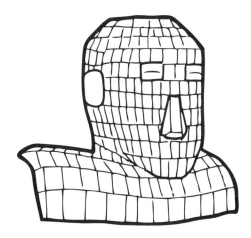

Directions
1. Cut the tissue paper into small squares.
2. Cut waxed paper into a shape—vase, disk, mask, animal figure, or urn.
3. Pour starch into cups and dilute slightly with water.
4. Lay overlapping pieces of tissue to cover the paper shape, lightly painting each piece as it is positioned with starch mixture.
5. Allow the starch to dry thoroughly. Trim the edges of the paper shape.

Embroidery

Embroidery is a craft with a long history in China. This type of stitchery was first used with the discovery of silk thread. Pillowcases, blankets, tablecloths, banners, altar cloths, clothing, fans, purses, shoes, and pictures are among the objects that are embroidered with traditional motifs such as birds, flowers, cats, and goldfish. Flowers, butterflies, and geometric designs decorate women's clothing, while dragons and bold, solid designs decorate men's. Elaborate pieces can take years and are often worked on by several people.

In early China, a girl's embroidery skills were thought to indicate whether she would make a good wife or not.

For the Teacher

Project

Use the technique of embroidery to create a design on fabric.

Materials

- blunt plastic or other stitchery needles
- various colors of embroidery floss
- scissors
- fabric squares
- embroidery stitch samples

Directions

1. Divide class into small groups. Assign each an adult volunteer.

2. Working one on one, teach students how to make a simple embroidery stitch. Copy the samples on this page for each student.

3. Once a simple stitch is mastered, students can complete the embroidery stitch pattern on their fabric square.

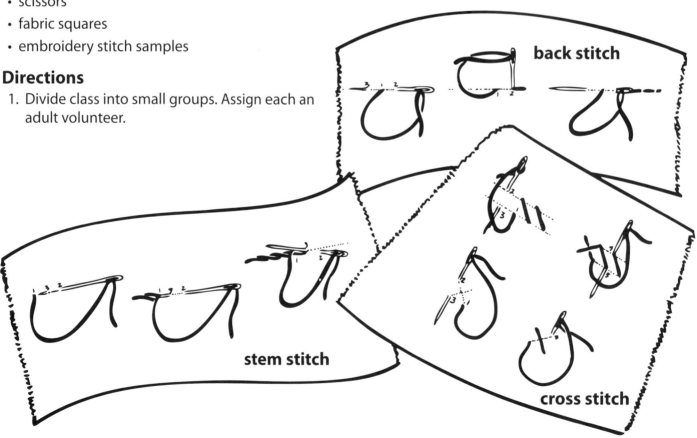

back stitch

stem stitch

cross stitch

Porcelain

The Chinese made the first porcelain during the Han dynasty. It became very popular during the T'ang dynasty, during which it was first exported. Sung dynasty potters then greatly improved the methods for making porcelain. But it was the Ming dynasty potters who produced the most elegant porcelain forms in lovely shades of green, blue, gray, and ivory to export to the West.

"Chinaware" differs from other pottery because of its whiteness. The decoration, or under-glaze, on the porcelain may be applied before the piece is coated with a glaze. The most reliable color is blue made from cobalt and seen in the earliest examples of Chinese porcelain. The secret of making Chinaware remained with the Chinese until the eighteenth century, when German potters finally figured it out.

Project

Paint a porcelain vase in the colors predominantly used in the earliest examples of Chinaware.

Materials

- blue and white construction paper
- blue watercolor paint and brushes
- scissors
- glue

Directions

1. Cut a vase shape from the white construction paper. Glue the vase to the blue construction paper backing.
2. Paint a design using blue watercolor paints or diluted tempera paint.

Time Line

Chinese history is divided into dynasties. Each dynasty is a period of time when one family was in power.

2000 B.C.–1500 B.C. **HSIA (XIA)**	1500 B.C.–1027 B.C. **SHANG**	1027 B.C.–221 B.C. **ZHOU (CHOU)**	221 B.C.–202 B.C. **CHIN**
• Dynasty of China is founded. • Potter's wheel is introduced. • Farming begins.	• Horse-drawn chariots are used. • Bronze weapons are cast. Silk is made. • Carving is done in jade and ivory. • Historical records are carved on tortoise shells.	• Multiplication tables are developed. • Casting of bronze and iron containers begins. • Confucius introduces his theories.	• Chopsticks are invented. • Great Wall is built. • Writing brush is used. • Weights and measures are standardized. • First emperor burns all books.
202 B.C.–A.D. 220 **HAN**	A.D. 220–A.D. 589 **THREE KINGDOMS**	A.D. 589–A.D. 618 **SUI**	A.D. 618–A.D. 960 **TANG**
• Confucianism becomes state religion. • Foot stirrups, paper, wheelbarrow, and the seismograph are invented. • The Silk Road opens for trade with Asia.	• China is divided into three kingdoms held by the kings of Wei, Shu, and Wu. • Buddhism increasingly influences the country.	• China is reunified during this short dynasty.	• Woodblock printing begins. • Porcelain is developed. • Highly cultural era; poetry and education flourish. • Gunpowder is invented.
A.D. 960–A.D. 1271 **SUNG**	A.D. 1271–A.D. 1368 **YUAN**	A.D. 1368–A.D. 1644 **MING**	A.D. 1644–A.D. 1912 **CHING**
• Magnetic compass is invented. • Gunpowder is used in fireworks. • Landscape paintings are produced. • Moveable type is invented	• Foreign travel is banned. • Great Wall is restored. • Marco Polo of Venice visits and takes news of China back to the world.	• Blue and white porcelain is produced. • Art and literature flourish.	• China expands to Tibet, Mongolia, and Central China. • Red and green pottery glazes are developed. • Peking Opera is established.

EP069 China © Highsmith® Inc. 2007

Literature List

Many other fine books on China are available. Ask your librarian for recommendations.

Bitter Dumplings
by Jeanne M. Lee. Farrar, Straus, and Giroux, 2002. 32 p. Gr. 1–4
After her father dies, a young Chinese woman struggles to survive and finds she has much in common with an old hunchbacked woman in her village.

Chu Ju's House
by Gloria Whelan. HarperCollins, 2004. 227 p. Gr. 5–6
In order to save her baby sister, 14-year-old Chu Ju leaves her rural home in modern China and earns food and shelter by working on a sampan, tending silk worms, and planting rice seedlings, while wondering if she will ever see her family again.

The Emperor's Silent Army: Terracotta Warriors of Ancient China
by Jane O'Connor. Viking, 2002. 48 p. Gr. 4–6
Describes the archaeological discovery of thousands of life-sized terracotta warrior statues in northern China in 1974.

Girls of Many Lands: Spring Pearl: The Last Flower
by Laurence Yep. Pleasant Company Publications, 2002. 224 p. Gr. 4–6
Called boyish by her new family for being able to read and write, 12-year-old, orphaned Spring Pearl's "odd ways" help save the family during the 1857 Opium War in Canton, China.

The Great Wall of China
by Lesley DuTemple. Lerner Publications, 2003. 80 p. Gr. 4–6
A history of the building of the various pieces of the Great Wall of China.

The Kite Rider
by Geraldine McCaughrean. HarperCollins, 2002. 272 p. Gr. 5–6
In thirteenth century China, after trying to save his widowed mother from a horrendous second marriage, 12-year-old Haoyou has life-changing adventures when he becomes a circus kite rider and ends up meeting the great Mongol ruler Kublai Khan.

Long Long's New Year
by Catherine Gower. Tuttle Publishing, 2005. 32 p. Gr. K–3
Long Long and his grandfather go to market to make money for their Spring Festival (Chinese New Year) celebrations.

Ms. Frizzle's Adventures: Imperial China
by Joanna Cole. Scholastic Press, 2005. 48 p. Gr. 1–5
From Chinatown, Ms. Frizzle and her tour group are transported to eleventh century China, where they learn how rice, tea, and silk are grown and harvested, and visit the Emperor in the Forbidden City.

Lon Po Po: A Red-Riding Hood Story from China
by Ed Young. Philomel Books. 1989. 32 p. Gr. 1–5
Three sisters staying home alone are endangered by a hungry wolf disguised as their grandmother. Caldecott Medal winner.

Shanghai Messenger
by Andrea Cheng. Lee & Low Books, 2005. 40 p. Gr. 3–6
A free-verse novel about 11-year-old Xiao Mei's visit with her extended family in China, where the Chinese–American girl finds many differences but also the similarities that bind a family together.

The Story of Kites
by Ying Chang Compestine. Holiday House, 2003. 32 p. Gr. K–2
Long ago in China, three brothers become tired of chasing birds from their family's rice fields and experiment with ways to make the job easier.

Glossary

bartering—trading goods and services without money

Buddha (Prince Siddhartha Gautama)—(c. 563–483 B.C.) "enlightened one," Indian philosopher who taught the way to personal enlightenment; founder of Buddhism

cai—food which is cut up into bite-size pieces

calligraphy—the art of decorative handwriting

Chung Kuo—middle country, the name that the Chinese call their country

Confucius—551–479 B.C., Chinese philosopher who taught obedience and ritual; founder of Confucianism

diviners—people who try to tell the future

dynasty—a line of rulers who come from the same family, sometimes lasting hundreds of years

embroidered—decorated with sewing designs

fan—grain

ideograph—symbols used to represent abstract ideas

lacquer—liquid that hardens to form a protective coating

lotus—a type of lily; symbol commonly used in Asian religions

Mah Jongg—Chinese game played with tiles engraved with Chinese drawings

Mao Zedong—Chinese communist party leader who founded the People's Republic of China (PRC), chairman of the PRC from 1949–1976

mein—Chinese noodles

oracle bones—ancient writings carved into animal bones; used for telling the future

People's Republic of China—founded in 1949 to replace the empire; led by the Chinese Communist Party

pictograph—symbols used to represent people and things

pi—disk

qigong—deep breathing exercises that can be focused to increase strength, decrease pain, and control disorders

sedan—a chair for one person carried between two strong poles by two male servants; wealthy families traveled in sedans during the Han and T'ang dynasties

tai chi chaun—deep breathing exercise combined with graceful circular movements

Weiqi—Chinese board game, known today as "Go"

wok—bowl-shaped frying pan

wushu—Chinese form of exercise fighting

zodiac—astrological signs